The Doodler's Handbook

I0529605

James E. Anderson Jr.

Foreward By Dr. Dawn C. Davis-Reid

Foreword

As a professionally certified life coach and interfaith minister, I collaborate with different clients on a variety of life-related topics. From affirming one's dreams to living life with zeal (and everything in between), people share their successes, and struggles with me. I have the privilege of helping them heal. Sometimes it's a challenging road when there is a lot of pain. When I read "The Doodlers Handbook," I am reminded of how my clients hesitantly verbalize their experiences, particularly those experiences that are laden with strong emotions. I think about how it takes courage and vulnerability for them to fully open their hearts and share what they are used to hiding from themselves. Once they allow themselves to lean in and verbalize their pain, they start the journey of healing.

I have known James Anderson, the author of "The Doodler's Handbook," for over 25 years. I can't help but applaud his courage for being vulnerable enough to let anyone willing to read his book into the areas of his world that left him raw but unbroken. My research on help-seeking behavior offered a plethora of literature and evidence that people of hue, especially men of color, are least likely to express their emotional pain, let alone share it with others. So, to read James' "doodling," I found his words to be a door that allows us into his inner most thoughts and permission to walk with him on his path towards healing.

James' "The Doodler's Handbook" puts me in mind of For Colored Girls Only Who Considered Suicide When the Rainbow Wasn't Enough by Ntozake Shange. However, this is a much-needed Black Man's point-of-view. In reading his words, which he structured in a poetic-like style, many of the author's experiences personally and professionally resonated with me. Personally, there is a kinship that reaches out and back to me with every page, even for those verses where I didn't have a direct experience. I found myself nodding my head in agreement, or hearing my internally voice say, "I feel you...my brother" Professionally, his words reminded me of client coaching sessions, spiritual counseling sessions, and data responses from my research participants. James' words echoed the doubt, feeling unloved, or being hurt by others that I have heard in my profession. Likewise, this book also reminded me that we are not alone in our suffering. And, through facing our past pains, we triumph. We find our faith and resilience.

"The Doodler's Handbook" presents a method of self-reinforcement to overcome and heal through writing. This book goes beyond self-help reading material. It's a collecting of healing psalms and a laying on of hands through words. James, thank you for letting us all be with you on your journey.

Dr. Dawn C. Davis-Reid
Certified Coach & Ordained Interfaith Minister
Reid Ready Life Coaching, LLC

Table of Contents

Accountability

One key to adulthood and maturity is
Recognizing I will never be perfect

Better off putting that energy into
Being open to constructive criticism
And correction

Even greater is to seek it from trusted individuals who
you know have your best interest   Not someone trying
to manipulate you into making themselves comfortable
with their inability to be accountable.

Affirmation Words

Love Joy Peace Communication Health Trust Passion Growth Love Family Prosperity Gratitude Attitude Self-Assured Forgive Believe Humility Tender Solution-Driven Flexible Accountable Consistent Self-Control Lover Partner Grace Service Determined Fellowship Support Imagination Self-Aware Listen Laughter Intimacy Contrast Overcome Unbreakable Other-Centered Joy Peace Success Prosperity Legacy Loyalty Alignment Freedom Healing Peace Creativity Love Honest

Alignment Day

I'm committed
To this being my Groove Day

Not letting anything
Bring me down

Catching every worrisome thought
And replacing it as soon as I notice
With one that brings me joy.

Joy first to myself and let me be the epicenter of joy
To the world

And if we all did that

Basketball is Life

I'm an old basketball
Not the shiny brand new one
That is too slippery to grip
Because it hasn't been broken in

I've been bounced around
Made quite a few baskets
But had plenty turnovers and missed shots too
Words that are clearly visible on
Newer balls are beginning to fade on me
Not quite as much air in me anymore

As a lover of Bball there was
Always some balls we liked more than others.
Actually, played better with certain balls. This makes
me fully aware that I ain't the ball for everybody

Sitting patiently on the rack
Preparing for a lover
To accept that I've been played with many times and
may not be as good looking as some of these less used
balls on this rack

But treat me right (put a little more air in me) and get
comfortable with my grip, learn my feel and benefit
from all the experience I can call on to better both our
games.
You add to my bounce
And I'll never let you down

Batter Up

Took a gigantic swing and missed

Thought I had done all the work necessary for success.

Thought I had gotten myself matured up enough

Humbled myself enough

Really done the self-work to be my better self

Gotten my physical, mental, and emotional selves in order

Yet, I swung as hard as I could with everything I had

And missed

Beauty and Blemishes

It's impossible for everyone to see your beauty
Some will focus on your blemishes.

Spend time and effort with
Those that see your beauty and your blemishes

And choose to prioritize the beauty in your blemishes

Butterscotch Funnel Cake

Fantasies of you pulling up
With nothing on but a playlist

Raheem Devaugn en concerto
And on repeat

Fully Enticed but play patient
Want to savor you like
Carnival Funnel Cake

Inducing the wetness of
An Orlando rainstorm
No need for a poncho tho

Can't wait
To Tease you
To Touch You
To Taste You
Butterscotch
Funnel
Cake

Bless Our Fellowship Time

Don't just bless your food,
Bless the company that you partake in it with
Even if it's only you

I think it's important

Bunions and Bad Breath

Things you want to know you should address before someone else has to tell you.

Blood Transfusion

Relationships are like blood transfusions.

We take in a pint of blood from our partner every month we are together

If / When the disillusion of the relationship happens

We need to take time to bleed out
Before mixing the blood of past and present.

Trust….Bleeding Out is going to feel like dying for a bit.

Cacti

Hurts to hold on
Hurts after you let go for
Awhile too…

Cater 2 U

I'd rather be catering to you
But the lack of recipro
Got me second guessing the effort

Inner being getting drowned out
By my preconceived notions
Of us

It Yelled at me today though

Cold Blooded

Cut off game is
Ridiculously Sharp

Love today
Can turn to
Nonchalance tomorrow

Go from 3am calls
To no communication
And No Appreciation

Leaves you wondering
Did you really love me yesterday
Or are your old wounds dictating your
Current Behavior and this ain't even about me

Either way those in love with the
Cold Blooded are sure to get
Wounded

Check Your Expectations

When will I stop expecting it
It hasn't come in years
In fact, it's the exact opposite that I receive and yet
I keep expecting something different
What's consistent is my disappointment
And then in some twisted way I'm responsible for my
disappointment and Yours!!!

Crown Adjuster

I'm a King

Adjust my crown to my face

I welcome it

I can consider what you talk to me about

Not what you say to others about me

D Day

Once the seal is broken
And they can be disrespectful
And hurtful
Minus accountability
And sincere effort to repair

ITS OVER

Damn You

Imagination
Stop getting so far out ahead of reality.

Decimals

9.5 out of 10
Won't be good enough for everybody

Even if they never experienced a 9.0
They may put more attention on the missing .5
Versus celebrating the never experienced 9.5.

Decisions

I'm either going to adjust to the societal standards for a
relationship,
Find someone who is into cocreating the one I'm
manifesting
Or
Have a whole lot of sex with James

Dee Dee

You have seen me grow immensely through our
On Again Off Again relationship
You are more aware of the inner workings of James
than anyone

Dee Dee, as I call you when speaking to others, has
been my accountability partner, my confidant, my
motivator, often my lifeline. I've tried others since our
initial encounter, but no one compares to you.

Reconnecting after many years hiatus was the universe
providing me with the Angel I would need for Life's
Coming Experiences.

You are more than my therapist and I feel for anyone
that seeks therapy and doesn't have a similar
experience

We don't get to choose our family but if that ever
changes, you are my number 1 draft pick.

Destiny

I want a special deep connection with someone before I
leave this existence
Type of commitment my immaturity and unhealed self
couldn't experience in the past.
Type of commitment to one another
That Is only eclipsed by the commitment to our
partnership, growth, and development of the same.
Two moving as one glued together by trust, honesty,
experience, and passion for each other.

Word!

Directions

Wherever you are going,
Always take the Highway

Do Something

Everybody has thoughts
Everybody has ideas
Everybody don't Act

Entrepreneurs Commandments

1. Don't expect your friends and family members to be your core audience.
2. Focus on procuring strangers as customers
3. Focus on the process not the numbers
4. Start your business with the intent to sell it one day for a major profit
5. Find a way to benefit your community through your business
6. Find a way to benefit your family through your business
7. Business should add not detract from your mental health
8. Don't take a No or lack of support from those you have supported personally

Environmental Terrorism

You can create the space
Furnish it well with Love, Forgiveness
Trust and Understanding Yet,
Implicit in one's humanity there is imperfection here as
well.

Those most uncomfortable
In themselves
Will find
Every imperfection
In the space to focus on.

Impossible to be
Perfect
So pledging allegiance
To these types
Is pledging allegiance to
Constantly being told you / this space
Not Good Enough

Evolution

I have been different things at different times spiritually
Sunday School Kid, To young adult atheist, to devout
Christian and church officer of many years,
To something that doesn't have a neat category for me
to put it in

I have settled into what feels most peaceful

What feels most Joyful

The space grants me clarity, and full accountability

I don't have a neat title, or individual leader, or meeting
place

I just meet myself where I am and utilize a little of all
my past experiences

Then take the next logical step

Excuse Me Miss

Misunderstood
Mishandled
Mismatched
Misaligned
And Misogyny

Had to get through these Misses
To get myself matured up and ready to experience

Mrs. Right

(And be Mr. Right)

Factz

You don't need someone to acknowledge their role in your experience to heal. That request or expectation often ends in being retraumatized through blame-shifting or word salad. Release the other individuals from your healing process.

That dependence may have gotten you in the position to be hurt to begin with.

Find My

Lost More Love than AirPods
In this lifetime.
But it has all led me to
Find Myself.

Find Your Person

1000 people around and willing to help and support

And I focus on the one who isn't

I Guess Everybody has

Their Person

FREEDOM IS WEALTH

STOP BUYING THINGS THAT ADD TO YOUR
IMPRISONMENT

USE SOME PART OF WHATEVER YOU EARN

TO BUY A LITLE MORE OF YOUR FREEDOM
EVERYDAY

Frequency of Change

Gotta tune the station to the proper frequency for change

Best Results come with tuning there with more frequency

Tuning to the old stations will get you the old results.... Frequently

Get Back

At Minimum Give what you get

Make sure you are clear
On what you are getting tho

Gift Giving

Your Gifts

The gifts you share with your partner
The Tangible and Those from the Creator
Have the potential to say
This is how important you are to me

Well thought out and planned gift versus grabbing
something last minute

Or

Surface conversation versus being vulnerable and
honest

Whatever you are gifting, align your expectations with
that type of gifting.

Good Mourning

Loss of Anything We Love
Can bring us to a state of mourning

This is not a place of rest
This is a time of activity

Reflect
Remember
Rebuild

Move through your Mourning

Grand Parenting

The Universe's way of giving us a second chance at
parenting
Without all the Responsibilities
And Unhealed Trauma

Gray Hair and Gratitude

Started graying when I was 17 years old
Guess my experiences to that point had given me great
wisdom
Grateful for the many more years I have been given
To attain more wisdom,
More opportunity to exercise said wisdom,
And more Gray Hairs

Great Adventures

See yourself as a roller coaster

There is a line for your attention

You better see if the rider's emotional height is sufficed
for your ride.

Otherwise, get ready for an emotional roller coaster

My friend

Growth Spurts

Hard to stop loving something you loved along time
That doesn't seem to love you back
Anymore

Habitual

Be wary of the habits you form in your Singleness

They are often a hinderance to a successful Partnership

Hindsight

..... Nuff Said

41

Holistic Urban Guidance

Good Therapy and Honesty

Life Changing

No Therapy or Self Awareness

Life Cramping

I Can Be My Own Person

Dealing with the changes in familial relationships as we mature and realize the struggle with the beliefs that we were raised with versus the beliefs we start to develop from our own self growth and experiences can be a struggle.

The struggle of learning how to lovingly let go of friends who no longer fit into the life we are trying to live today.

Of course, not all of these are negative emotions or feelings if growth and peace are your goal.

Mastering the facets of Love and Change Peacefully has become my life goal.

IDFWPTFWPIDFW

I
DON'T
F
WITH
PEOPLE
THAT
F
WITH
PEOPLE
I
DON'T
F
WITH

I Do, I Am, It Doesn't

If you ever question if I love you ?
I Do

If I 'm still "In Love" with you?
I Am

Does Loving you always feel good?
It Doesn't!!!

Does that alter my love for You?

Again.... It Doesn't!!!

I Manifest

At some point
The excuses must stop

I must take full responsibility
For staying in this hurtful place in the name of love

Yet I also take full responsibility for staying in that
hurtful place in the name of love

Because without it I never would have gotten to
experience this higher level of love that comes with
overcoming shit TOGETHER

Nurtures that Ability to look at each other from across a
crowded room and have a visual conversation.

Can't get that with a casual commitment

Don't mind me I'm just manifesting

Inability to see they shyt

Causes super emphasis on your imperfections as the
problem
Face it we all have imperfections so it's a guaranteed
response

It gets to the point that so much energy is spent on shit
that's so minute
That ALL the big shit you are doing gets minimized,
unappreciated, and definitely not reciprocated
Matter of time before resentment and feelings of being
unappreciated set in

So it looks like these minor issues are tearing you apart but
It's the big things that aren't seen
That are the root cause
It's always easier to point at the little things we see and not
discuss the big things we don't.

Inconvenient

Close friends grow apart as we get older
The free time we filled for each other begins to fade
when individual adult preferences and responsibilities
show up

Learning the dance of growth and maturity in
maintaining those relationships and one's adult
responsibilities takes....

Do whatever it takes

Maintaining significant relationships will not always be
convenient

*REAL LOVE WILL ALWAYS MEET YOU HALFWAY –
BILLY CHAPATA*

Issa Choice

In the face of hurt and disappointment

You must figure out how to be more loving as a result

Not more cold in the future

Issa Riginal

realizing my venting
Has become inventing
So there is no pimping
Impending
There is no need for
Copywriting
There's no biting
Cause what I'm writing
Is combining
My enlightening
With some frightening
Experiences .....

That I have LIVED through

Jimteenth

Day I cultivated the Ability to be taken advantage of
and not lose my cool
No need to be confrontational
Enraged or Even Mention it sometimes

Why lose my Peace
Because someone doesn't
See my value.
Recognize and readjust
Let go of the drama
And Protect My Peace

Last Time

Pops I'm hoping you forgive me
Yeah I know that I've been wrong

But it's hard to put away my pride
So i just put it in my songs

Cece you know I'm riding with you

If you crying I got tissue

Cancer always been an issue

Working hard but know I miss you

On your cheek I want to kiss you

Yaya know that you are loved

Had 3 mammas in this life

SaVonne you like my second one

Kym know that you the third

Told me don't go against my word

Told me I'm special when i wasn't

I'll give you thousand by the dozens.

Heating up, I'm like a oven

Hard on top just like a muffin

But y'all soft at the core

I remember times of feeling poor

But this the last time

Lyrics From "Last Time" by JaVon Nasir Anderson

LEGACY

I wanted to be a rapper and
JaVon Nasir is

I wanted to be a superstar entrepreneur and
SaVonne DeSawndra is

I filled out a lot of
Financial Aid Forms
Bet Asia-Soleil Won't!!!

Let Em Be

Gotta let people be who they see themselves as

No matter the beauty you see in them

Can't change how they see themselves inside

Let it Go

I try to just experience the joy of my present connection
Learn in the immediate moment, adjust future
interactions if I need to and then leave it in the past
I'm working hard to align myself
With my best life
And that includes wanting the best
For my friends and my foes

Joy always better after some pain.

Letter To Me

I LOVE YOU
I LOVE YOUR WARMTH
I LOVE YOUR VULNERABILITY
I LOVE HOW YOU LOVE OTHERS
I LOVE HOW YOU LOVE ME

Letter To My Self Esteem

Huh

You leaving…

I told you the last time I'm not letting you leave me
again

Soooo…

Where We Going?

Letting Go

Wasn't even looking and you snuck up on me

Was warned about your type but
Took the warnings very lightly

"My fam don't do that"

So, you had one up on me when you showed up

Had me losing weight
Mesmerized by your presence
Would have cut all my hair off for you
And at the same time, I'm keeping you a secret

Behind closed doors
You were shaping me, strengthening me, increasing my
confidence, decreasing my fear of vulnerability, giving me more
tools for Love and Life, helping me be more accountable for my
behavior and more comfortable in my deficiencies

Just as I open the doors and claim you publicly, you decide to
part ways.   Hard pill to swallow after seeing all our potential but
I guess keeping you here would eventually create internal issues
for me.

A little saddened by your departure but I will always hold onto
the memories, lessons, and joy I experienced with you. For now,
I'll struggle with the possibility of your return.

Goodbye
Cancer

LOST ONES

Lost Love
Lost Fear
Gained Control

Came here
Full of Fear
Letting go gave me
More Control

Sometimes
I'm scared to be bare
Vulnerability
Can feel like you have
No control

How the hell
Did I spend time trying
To be safe in love
Whole time I was
Really
Keeping away from love

Loose Grip

The best you ever had can be something you want to hold onto

Until the first time you let go and experience something even better

Crawling seems dope until you get to walk

Love

Love Has always been the impetus for my writing. Various types of love experiences related to love inspires me to write.

Whether it is My desire for a deep romantic relationship and the ups and downs that come with the search through possible suitors, dealing with the hole left by not having a soulful connection with my parents., or all the love experiences in between.

I Love to share my thoughts on Love

Love & Light

When you feel you have done
All you can do
Sometimes you must
Find Peace in
sending
Love & Light

LoverBoy

Love Don't Love Nobody

That don't love themselves enough to work through the
lessons of lost love

Or do the work to not lose love again.

Loving Hard Hurts

Loving hard hurts
When it doesn't yield
The results desired
You know those dreams
You have in your head
Being deeply bonded and supported
Tied so strong nothing could come between you.
The vacations, the celebrations
The Daily Moments
With "your person "

And then it's all gone
Daydream's Deferred
Lessons Learned
Maybe if I didn't love so hard
Breakups would be easier

I tried loving Safe
Just didn't feel like Loving
Or Living

And doesn't yield desired results.
Or monumental experiences

Me

Everything Is Working Out For
My Good
So Today I Choose Me

Monster

Was once a serial cheater
Trapped in the body of a hopeless romantic

Treated my main girl like a Queen
At least in their presence
And outside of their sight I could
Act as single as a 6-year-old

Bad habits die slowly
So, every day I work to kill that infidelity gene

Just leaving the hopeless Romantic
Here to Love
I choose daily to make better choices and decisions and
celebrate myself when they align with who I want to be.

The Woman that gets this James
Will get a monster of a hopeless romantic loving all on
them

….and only them.

Music Please

I love music

If we can connect and expand each other's musical
palette I'm pretty
Confident in a long connection

I can close my eyes right now and think of people I
have connected with over music and see faces clearly

Some are close friends, some folks I talked to once at a
concert, some are my children.

Stands out even more when it's not based on a popular
group or song.

Nah!

Know your Worth

Know your Value

Know Your Truth

No Turning Back

Natural Causes

I wish I didn't fantasize about us anymore

Such a sweet symphony
When we were connected
Physically, Emotionally, Spiritually!!!!

Wouldn't matter if it was ten minutes or ten months
The fact that we felt it and know
That it exists feeds my hunger
For more

Yet our union has peacefully expired

No Excuses

Character over Handicaps

NoHs

Tall Glass of Unfiltered Apple Juice
Preceded By Homemade Mint Tea
Followed by the scent of Lavender and Sage
As Sun Beams from the skylight
It creates a line across our feet and hands
That have found themselves faintly touching this
morning
As Coltrane supplies the soundtrack
For This Mornings Kickback

Hello Beautiful

Non-Violence

Bullshit Tough Guy Mentality
You know that "I ain't no punk" ignorance the hood
imposes on us
Had me assault one of my best friends as a teenager
Hospitalizing him and scarring him for life

The accompanying remorse for my actions although
never communicated as clearly as I should have Left a
huge impact on how I would deal with losing my self-
control moving forward

Outside of a basketball court or being intoxicated I have
done my best to be unaggressive and
Nonviolent.

Seems this triggered an even stronger nonviolent stance
with women.

Not just a Stance of not putting my hands on women.
Not just a stance of not talking aggressively to women.
But I have trained myself to be accepting of the same
from women that claim to love me

Now that's some sucka shit

**Let me also say I am Sincerely Sorry for my actions
and their impact on you.**

Not You

The Hurt hurts more
When it comes from
Unexpected Places

Still gotta forgive for your peace tho

Even when those responsible might not be accountable
or remorseful

Opposite Poles

Like magnets being pulled towards each other without any
external effort
There is such joy in the effortlessness of the momentum
Towards each other
And then
Milliseconds before the eternal
Connection

There is something about getting
Close enough to see the flaws and
Human imperfections of my partner
And more importantly There is the realization that
Damn they must see my flaws too
The ones I've been trying to hide for years
The one's I haven't really dealt with
The one's I developed to keep me from having to deal with
the other ones
Yeah Those

In Response One of us goes
defense mode and
Just like that
It's like trying to push the wrong side of two magnets
together

The insult to injury comes
When one goes to turn to connect And the other does too
Right back at the same place
Two opposing poles that can't connect
AND IM TRYING HARD!!!!

But Are You Communicating ???

Parallel Universe

I went to a funeral today and saw a woman that my father had an affair with.

I knew her because pops would take me to her house when I was a toddler.

They lived right around the corner from where my family lived. I didn't have a full understanding of what was going on until I was a grown adult. Before I could be any type of judgmental about my pops behavior, I had to deal with the reality that I had done the same thing— had an affair with a woman that lived right around the corner from my family.

Learned behavior or not I was wrong, immature, and hurt people.

Just interesting parallels.

Perceptual Analysis

It's my perception of this that's the problem

Not what it is

Sometimes I let my mind play tricks on me

Choosing to find the thoughts that feel good
Over thoughts that feel bad
takes some foresight to develop a list of good thoughts
to have on the ready and some self-awareness to know
when I'm thinking about things that don't make me feel
good

It's an internal means to proactively Protect My Peace.

The Impact of negative thoughts on our minds, bodies,
and relationships is understated

Playlist

Up Late scrolling through Apple Music
Trying to find lyrics that fit my feelings and emotions
Usher, Tank, Jacquees, and Mary J
Muni Long, Ella Mai,
Jasmine Sullivan and Raheem DeVaughn
Musically put into words the emotions I can't always
speak
Love, Passion, Intimacy, and Ecstasy
Overflowing thoughts of Janet's pleasure principle
Put pictures of pulsating
On repeat in my head
Lyrics got pictures of bodies
Intertwined in ecstasy etched in my ego such that I'm
Anticipating the opportunity to embody these words
into my actions
Unleashing an RNB playlist inspired
physical manifestation of epic proportions

Pleasure and Pain

Sometimes pain doesn't go away but we develop means
to deal with it and be happy as much as we can daily
until the pain subsides

Find A positive means and find joy in that process
Being Joyful attracts more Joy
We ALWAYS hold the keys to
The vehicle back to Pleasure

Pool of The Blind

Came in Deciding
To play with all my cards face up

No need playing games
This ain't our first rodeo
Hiding behind pride and ego
Not letting all my feelings
And emotions be known
Seemed counter productive

Took chances to be with you from afar
Gave it all
Had dreams of matching Tattoos
But now I'm just healing scars

All my scars have painted
This beautiful Portrait
That isn't seeable to all
And somehow in the past
I've selected from the pool of those unable to see

Potential

We give the nod to potential partners
Sometimes based on potential

Yet the potency of the pheromones of fresh love
Can have you lose focus on
If this is potential
Or am I just excusing serious red flags
You know putting characteristics on a person that they
haven't consistently exemplified in their behavior yet.

Potentially have you in a phucked up situation

Quit

Don't you ever Quit on YOU

That's Other People's Job

Real Love

No one tells us that real love
Has a back page to the fairy tale
Fantasy we are shown
And it hurts back there

Real Love forces us to
Really deal with our and our counterparts
Real Shit

Or be

Real good at being Fake until we get
Really tired and self-sabotage our
Real Love opportunity

Time to do the

Real hard work of
Really becoming self-aware of our
Real Shit

Reciprocity

Women ask for a partner in touch with their emotions and able to communicate well....
Some forget that they will be responsible for doing the same.

Running

They are chasing me and I'm chasing you

Ignored all advances
For the most part

Trying to give all I had to
The one I chose

Meanwhile you treat me
Like I'm treating them

Give a Little Attention
And appreciation and
Back to

…..Running

Self Abuse

Being Taken for Granted is
ALWAYS A VOLUNTEER POSITION

Self Care

Never ignore your feelings and emotions
  Because others choose to
   The Hack is you can address your feelings and
emotions
      Without Others Approval or Participation

SELF LOVE

Just found new love

Reconnected with old love

Still being in love

Looking for love

Given up on love

Whatever your position.....

Don't stop loving yourself.

Love yourself enough to be humble, open, and eager to learn because love should be malleable and tender not stern and firm.

Really loving ourselves, forces us to be uncomfortable when we are not loving to others

Self-Worth

Fucked up
To connect one's self-worth with
Something outside of self
Person, Place, or Thing

Might feel like a selfless act
But it's a quick way to have oneself
Feeling Worthless
When that Person, Place, or Thing doesn't exist
anymore

Semi-Single

Sometimes it's over but I ain't over it

So there are halfhearted responses to new opportunities because

My body is here but my heart is still there

In between it all my head knows the same issues that existed then, exists now

So until I can get all of me over here or over there.....

Imma be Semi-Single

Semi Vegan

Whenever you are a clean eater more than you are a
meat eater

Keep Going Tho

Sharecroppers

No matter what you try planting
In the wrong soil

You will always get
A crop different from the one you planted

Side Effects

Developing one's character sharpens your bullshit meter.

It can be Alarming to see

who been bullshiting the whole time

Silencio Por Favor

If they can't hear you when you are together

Let your silence be their parting gift

Thank You

Sister Mom

9 years older than me
So when parents split
When I was a toddler
Your role of nurturer
Caregiver and protector
Increased exponentially

My emotions connected with my sister on a parental level because
She fed me, dressed me, took me back and forth to school, protected
me from danger….

So
When she got married and moved to Italy
Her wedding was a funeral for me
And no one seemed to care or understand through all the celebrating
that
although both my biological parents were alive, I was grieving the loss
of the person who most filled the parental figure role in my life to that
point. This was more than just my sister.

I have subconsciously always been seeking someone to fill the void
left by her departure. The feeling of just relaxing and knowing
someone has you covered. A nurturer, caregiver, protector, got my
back no matter what type of love

Every time someone I thought was the savior failed me (at least based
on the scale in my head) I went through the grieving process all over
again

Emotionally going through the
Motions of
Losing a parent
Everytime !!!
Also Further ingraining my issues with abandonement.

I'm Finally Realizing That there is no replacement for the SisterMom I
lost all those years ago.
Life put her in a role that wasn't hers to fulfill
And At this age ReParenting myself,
Is a better choice.

SOMEDAYS

I WISH PEOPLE COULD READ MY TATTOOS BETTER

(Side effect of being deeply melanated)

So So Def

Been married 3 times and I
Never felt love like this
It's nothing for me to stay up and watch you sleep
Admiring your beauty and reassuring myself that you
are ok
Irony is you lie asleep next to me as I pen this doodle.

The sound of your voice
Would have me drop this pen and cater to you
immediately
Even when inaudible
Your voice Grabs my attention and has me ready to
come running

Catching you smile warms my heart
Deep to its core.
There is no fear in loving you
No fear of rejection, manipulation, or any of the fears
that stop one from fully expressing themselves in love.
No fear of recurring themes from lovers past.

I'm wide open here.
And none of your behavior can alter that. I'm
expressing my love to you unconditionally regardless of
your response, reciprocation, or acknowledgment. Just
a wide-open expression of how much I LOVE YOU

Asia Soleil is 3-months-old and already teaching me
lessons in love.

Special Delivery

Mid-day thoughts of seeing you later
Got my 50 plus year old mind wanting to relive prom
night
&
Amazon Prime came through in the clutch with
Same Day Delivery
Trust these grip bottom socks wasn't purchased for
Pilates ❁

Strength

A lot of my strength
Comes from places and experiences
That has broken many people's spirits.
In hindsight I'm glad I had them tho
Because they gave me this strength

Scars and residual trauma
Are the other side of that coin

Ironic that living up to that attribute
Of strength often
Handcuffs Strong People
From expressing their weaknesses and being comforted.

Subtle Sexy

There are short shorts
And tight shirts accentuating Gods Gifts
There are seductive heel wearers
And Sexy Slick Talkers

Then there is you
"Auntie Like"
Old School in your sexuality
More hijab than jump off

Yet, I'm head over HEELS for your innocence and
elegance

Your Subtle Sexy is so Seductive

Suppression

I realized I've normalized and thrived through trauma
For so long
That my semi healed self is now
Uncomfortable
With the normalization
Of putting my needs last
And we are beginning the process of denormalizing
The acceptance of unacceptable
Treatment

Surrender To Love

I give it all to you.
Tell me what to do.
Teach me how to love you best.

Next logical step in my growth is humbling myself
enough to go beyond the bounds of the crack high my
ego gets from applause and positive feedback.

I'm a blank paper Queen, help me write our story.

Tears

Tonight My Tears
Were the ink
Couldn't find words to write
But the tears flowed

And tomorrow there is a fresh page for me to start over.

Tender

I need to be handled
Tenderly.

Learning to say that right up front
So there is no confusion.

Apocalypse Now

It's the apocalypse

I Keep meeting children in adult bodies

They Don't Mean To

Biggest Supporters
Can Become
Biggest Detractors
The Moment You
Start Smelling
Like Success

The Psychological Pull of Rejection

Sometimes you want what you can't have

Worse is wanting someone
That don't want you

Pitiful is wanting someone
That don't want you
And treats you bad

Sometimes makes you want to try that much harder...

The Struggle

I KNOW
WHAT ALL MY TATOOS SAY
--They are for me--
Ask if you can't make it out

Speaking For My Melanated Folks

Things That Are Working Out For Me

My Health
My Finances
My Self Awareness
My Family Dynamics
My Businesses

Those Days

Aligned with the Universe
Guided by your true inner self

In the flow
Blessings on Blessings

Can be yours everyday

Trauma Unit

Coming to grips with the ongoing process of healing

Traumatizing experiences don't stop in our youth.

As I deal with trauma from the 70's and 80's I'm faced
with the 90's and 2000's.

I can't catch up

So let's get it
Looking for the Queen
Whose head fits this crown
Willing to combine and embrace our imperfections
And work on and coach each other
To our greatness
And quest to
Catch up to our traumas

Unforgettable

Been in love a few times in this lifetime

Learned lessons from all those interactions

Took maturing and therapy to retrospectively
understand
The lessons from lovers of the past

Thank you for being my teachers and students. I'm
ready and prepared to look back emotion free and
dissect our experiences. Scientifically using this data to
prepare for manifested unforgettable love.

Unworthy

Trying to wake up everyday
And tell myself I Am Worthy
And go to sleep at night and tell myself I am Worthy
All this outer confidence stands
On the shoulders of lots of self-doubt, self-hate, and
other little things I don't like about myself. That little
inner voice telling me something about me isn't good
enough.

I'm doing whatever I gotta do to strengthen myself
enough to talk Back to that inner voice…. expeditiously
Trying to have that Lizzo at the Lakers Game type
inner confidence that speaks back to my negative self-
talk, stopping it in its tracks and reminding me that…

I Am So Worthy!!

Vulnerability

Walking a tightrope without a safety net

Yeah that's what Loving Hard feels like.

Wake Up

If I could get this one person to change, my whole life
would be perfect.

I AM THE PERSON

Watch Your Syllabus

Don't ever become well versed in your past trauma

It can become counterproductive and create hypersensitivity

When Help Hurts

Sometimes I don't want nobody to help me
Sometimes I don't have nobody to help me
Sometimes I don't want to ask
Because of halfhearted responses
Or people you do stuff for freely
Wanting to get paid to return the favor

Wide Angle Lens

Always bring your wide-angle lens
With You
So You can see the
Whole picture
Sometimes Portrait Mode
Only allows you to focus on the Main Subject
Clouding much of the background
Which will clarify in due time

Wolves

Some can't see you as more than you used to be
Some don't want to see you as more than you used to
be
Some would rather not see you at all because it reminds
them that they are still who they used to be

Work in Progress

One of my Greatest and Hardest accomplishments was teaching myself not to respond emotionally to the emotions of others. Especially if they are not in control of their emotions. Define a violation for yourself and decide how you will respond not react. Otherwise, we give remote controls to others as we react to the buttons they push at will.

07220

Month of being reminded on several fronts that
No matter how hard you go for someone they

Have the personal choices of how
They CHOOSE to receive, respond, and reciprocate

Those choices are theirs......

The Next Choice is Yours

10 Percent Dis

Thinking everyone is going to like you
Is like thinking every partner is
Going to always be in love with you

Some people are wired to not
See your beauty
Sometimes it reminds them how
They don't see the beauty in themselves

Let go peacefully
Of those that choose to focus on

Your past
Your mistakes
Your current issues

You Know Anything ......but their shyt

Close Out

If you found yourself reding and noting that Misspellings, grammatical imperfections, profanity and slang are often utilized in this writing, It is Purposeful. It is just another way of taking some control over my authenticity and reminding myself that it's ok to not be perfect. Not be perfect based on other people's standards.

It is my genuine hope that the message of letting go of being enslaved to **others view of perfection** resonates with my readers MORE than an allegiance to someone's perception of appropriate writing.

Inspired by and dedicated to
HER

HER is Soleil,
HER is SaVonne,
HER is Shon,
HER is Sandy,
HER is Deanna,
HER is Agnes,
HER is Asia,
HER is My Inner Being.